THE THREE GIFTS:

The Truth about Santa Claus

by M.P. Ilse

The Three Gifts: The Truth about Santa Claus
Copyright © 2013 by M.P. Ilse
All rights reserved.

No part of this publication may be reproduced, stored in a retrieval system or transmitted in any form by any means, electronic, mechanical, photocopy, recording, or otherwise, without the prior permission of the publisher, except as provided by USA copyright law.

Scripture taken from the *New American Standard Bible©*, Copyright © 1960, 1962, 1963, 1968, 1971, 1972, 1973, 1975, 1977, 1995 by The Lockman Foundation. Used by permission.

Cover art by Dane B. Low

ISBN-13: 978-1492862178
ISBN-10: 1492862177

To BBS, ACS, and JAS, with love and gratitude.

A Note to My Readers

Is Santa Claus real?

This book is born of a question, a question to which there is no easy "Yes" or "No" answer. How can one sum up the Spirit of Christmas – something that has been in existence in one form or another for over *two thousand years* - with a one-word answer? It started with the quiet birth of a baby, was kept alive by devoted followers of a divine teacher, and is now celebrated worldwide in a vast variety of ways.

When my own son asked me if Santa Claus were real, I told him I would look into it, and began to research the question. As a person searching for an answer to a question, I did as most people do today: I turned to the internet. I did not find what I considered to be a *good answer*. Instead, I found dusty old history lessons, extremely fanciful websites for small children, and thoughtless bloggers who carelessly plopped out too-easy answers in much the same way as the cafeteria lady plops cold mashed potatoes onto your tray. Dissatisfied, I kept researching.

A very good attempt to answer the question well came from an editorial published in 1897 in a New York newspaper called the *Sun*. Believing that anything written in the *Sun* was the absolute truth, a young girl named Virginia had written a letter to the editor, asking him whether Santa Claus is real. The *Sun* editor's answer to young Virginia is a very good one (look it up sometime!) but was lacking in facts, and it was missing some important, real-life parts of the story behind who Santa Claus *really is*. I kept researching, and from information I found within many websites, books, and articles, I finally made some discoveries and connections that I am satisfied with. Is Santa Claus real? This book is my answer to the question.

What I realized is that there *is* a good answer based in factual people and events, but it will take time to explain. For you to *really* understand the answer, you need some background information. To know who Santa Claus *really* is, you must first understand what Christmas really is, and hear the two-thousand-year-old story that starts with a baby's birth and continues on still, today. And, as always, in order to understand the whole story, one must start at the very beginning. So if you truly want to know if Santa Claus is real, be patient and read on!

The First Gift:

The Very First Christmas

To understand who *Santa Claus* really is, it is important to first understand what *Christmas* really is. Young Americans today would probably define the Christmas "season" (which seems to start earlier and earlier every year) as a time when people shop for gifts in decorated stores and then wrap them in order to give to their friends and family on Christmas day. Children whisper their wish-lists into the ears of department-store Santas, and the desired items magically appear under the tree on Christmas morning. Families travel to visit one another, gifts are exchanged, big meals are shared, and school is out for over a week. Hurray!

But there's another, more subtle Christmas tradition that also takes place every year: Many people go to church on Christmas Eve or on Christmas Day, and sometimes people put up "nativity scenes" – little or big (or even live) models and reenactments of a stable room featuring wise men, animals, an angel perhaps, a mother and a father, and a newborn baby called Jesus sleeping in a manger. Although many holiday songs tell of Santa, reindeer, elves, and the pure fun of the season, other Christmastime songs tell of Jesus' birth, of an ancient city called Bethlehem, angels, and of a precious gift that was given that first Christmas night.

Two different celebrations: one of Santa Claus and shopping for gifts, and one of a small baby born long ago… which tells of the *real* Christmas? Truly, the holiday that we call Christmas is based on a long-standing annual celebration of the birth of Jesus; without Jesus, there would *be* no Christmas.

So who exactly is Jesus, anyway, and why is His story so important in defining Christmas?

The Very First Christmas

From the beginning of time, cultures all over the world have believed in the existence of a "higher power," a supernatural god who reigns over the earth and the human beings who live on it. As a matter of fact, three major religions in the world - Islam, Judaism, and Christianity - believe in the *same* God (although they have different names for Him) and generally agree about the very beginnings of God's relationship with the human race.

Christmas, however, is a tradition that sets Christians apart from Muslims and Jewish people. Christians believe that God has a son whom He sent to earth in human form many years ago, to help people understand Him and how He would like people to live their lives on earth. This son's name was Jesus. Christians believe he was "the Christ" (a title that means "chosen one") and therefore often call Him *Jesus Christ*.

To celebrate Jesus Christ's birthday, some Christian churches traditionally held (and still hold) a service called a *mass*, and that is how the annual celebration of Christ's birth came to be called *Christmas*.

The birth of the baby Jesus was a gift to humankind. God had promised this gift to His people centuries before Jesus' actual birth, and many people had anxiously awaited that gift for centuries. People who trusted in God at that time were often oppressed by other nations, religions, and cultures, and they longed for a time when they could live as free people in a land of their own, worshipping the God that their ancestors worshipped. Their holy writings (what we know as the Old Testament of the Bible) spoke of a savior or *Messiah* whom God would provide to lead them into a better life, a life that was more like the life God wanted them to lead.

Prophets (people who were believed to be messengers of God's word) spoke of a baby to be born who would become the Messiah (also known as the Christ) and gave predictions as to where the birth would take place and who His family would be. A prophet named Isaiah foretold the following description about Jesus, centuries before Jesus was actually born:

> *For a child will be born unto us, a son will be given to us;*
> *And the government will rest on His shoulders;*
> *And His name will be called Wonderful Counselor, Mighty God, Eternal Father, Prince of Peace.*
> *There will be no end to the increase of His government or of peace,…*

Believers anxiously awaited the birth. When Jesus was actually born, though, it was a quiet affair. Most people had no idea that the birth had taken place. One of the best descriptions of Jesus' birth – the very first Christmas – appears in the Bible and was written by Luke, a writer and believer who personally knew Jesus. Here is Luke's version of the story of the very first Christmas:

> *While they were there, the days were completed for [Mary] to give birth.*
> *And she gave birth to her firstborn son; and she wrapped Him in cloths, and laid Him in a manger, because there was no room for them in the inn.*
> *In the same region there were some shepherds staying out in the fields and keeping watch over their flock by night.*
> *And an angel of the Lord suddenly stood before them, and the glory of the Lord shone around them. And they were terribly frightened.*
> *And the angel said to them, Do not be afraid, for behold, I bring you good news of great joy which will be for all the people;*
> *For today in the city of David there has been born for you a Savior, who is Christ the Lord.*

Why did the angel call Jesus a "Savior"? For people who believe that Jesus was a gift to humankind from God, His *birth* was a very special event in Christian history. But here's an important idea -- Jesus' *death* is a much, much more important story:

We all know that there is good and evil in every human's heart. We are all capable of doing very *good* things -- such as showing love for one another, sharing possessions, showing compassion to those who are troubled or hurt, or volunteering time and talents to help people or a community. Sadly, we also are all very capable of doing *bad* things – such as being selfish or hurting others with our words or actions. This human tendency to do evil is called *sin*, and people have been troubled by their own sin since humans first walked the earth and recognized that both good and evil existed.

As we all know, when we sin, we feel guilty; sometimes an apology will make us feel better, and sometimes we try to lessen our guilt by doing or saying good things to "make up" for the bad thing we've done. Guilt hurts our hearts until we feel that we have been forgiven in some way. Before Jesus was born, people asked God for forgiveness by giving money to their temple, or by giving up a valuable possession or animal. But then people would simply go out and sin again; sadly, sinning seems to be part of human nature. The method of seeking forgiveness through giving up money or possessions didn't seem to be working enough to make people *want* to stop sinning.

God realized that people needed to feel a closer relationship to Him, and they needed an easier (and more permanent) method of finding forgiveness when they sinned. For that reason, and because God loves humankind more than we can ever imagine, God gave us the ultimate gift: Jesus Christ. Jesus was His Son, God in human form, someone whom people could meet, touch, listen to, and learn from. Someone who could personally teach people about the lives

God wanted them to live. Perhaps with this real-life teacher living among them and modeling godly behavior, people could feel closer to God and get a better idea about how God wanted them to live, think, and act.

For thirty-three years Jesus walked the earth, teaching and loving, inspiring followers, helping the poor and sick, and changing lives. As a gift to us from God, He changed humankind by being a living, breathing example of how to live, think, and believe in a way that pleases God and avoids sin. He also modeled forgiveness by spending time with people who sinned and inspiring all but the most stubborn to try to change their sinful ways. Jesus was unconditional in His love; He believed that all people were worthy of His love and forgiveness, no matter what they had done before they got to know Him. He also taught that all sin could be forgiven, as long as the sinner continued to try to believe in Jesus and live a life worthy of His love.

The Forever Gift: Jesus' Death and What It Means

Providing us with a real-life teacher and model of holiness and forgiveness was just one way that Jesus was a gift from God. Christians believe that Jesus' *death* was a second way that Jesus was a gift to us from God: Before Jesus, people sacrificed money and possessions to be forgiven for sins, but when Jesus died, He *became* the ultimate sacrifice to gain forgiveness for the sins – *all sins, all over the world, from the beginning of time to the end of time, once and for all* – of all humankind.

Jesus' friend and follower Peter said it best, speaking to people (then and now) who want to have a good relationship with God:

For Christ also died for sins once for all, the just for the unjust, so that He might bring us to God…

Jesus died on a cross, took punishment that he didn't deserve for OUR sake, instead of us, to bring about eternal forgiveness for us. When we understand that and feel grateful for it, it helps us to try not to sin, and to remember that when we DO sin, God loves us anyway and trusts us to try to do better. This knowledge takes away the guilty feeling that makes us feel dead and hopeless inside, and helps us to remember that we will always be loved by God, even after we die.

And Jesus' friend John explained **why**:

> *For God so loved the world, that He gave his only begotten Son, that whoever believes in Him shall not perish, but have eternal life.*

Jesus knew that by sacrificing His own human life, He was earning forgiveness for us and for our sins. He said to his followers (and to us, in the Bible) that if you accept His gift, you will never truly die; even when your body dies, your soul will continue to live in Heaven with God. Jesus told His friend Mary,

> *I am the resurrection and the life; he who believes in Me will live even if he dies, and everyone who lives and believes in Me will never die.*

Three days after Jesus' physical body died on the cross, He came alive again (this is called the *Resurrection*; Christians celebrate this each year on Easter Sunday as a remembrance of how Jesus rescues believers from sin and death). Jesus continued to teach and inspire His followers for another forty days after His resurrection. When He finally left them to return to Heaven, He filled His followers with a "heavenly spirit" that gave them special understanding of why He lived and died, and how best to teach people all over the world about the amazing gift that God offered humankind by sending Jesus to live and die for us. His followers then spent the rest of their lives spreading the "good news" around the world, and writing about it so that people throughout the rest of time would be able to learn about Jesus Christ, God's greatest gift to all of us.

The Second Gift:

Saint Nicholas

For many years after Jesus died, only a few people understood who He really was, and what His life (and death) meant to humankind. Jesus' followers did as they promised, spreading out across Europe, Asia, and the Middle East, telling everyone who would listen to them about Jesus' life and teachings. Because they believed in Jesus Christ, Jesus' followers called themselves "Christians." Some listeners rejected the news about Christ, but many others believed, and those believers helped to spread the news further throughout the world. The Roman Empire (which ruled much of this area in those first few centuries after Jesus' birth and death) at first rejected the Christian story. Representatives of the Roman Empire imprisoned, tortured, or killed many Christians who attempted to spread the news of Jesus' gift; however, that changed dramatically in the year 313 A.D., with the unlikely help of a very important person in that world: the Emperor of the Roman Empire.

The Emperor of the vast and all-powerful Roman Empire was a man called Constantine I, whose mother considered herself a Christian. In the year 313 A.D., Emperor Constantine decided that the persecution of Christians was wrong, and passed a law that allowed people of his empire to worship whomever they liked, however they liked. With his power and money, Emperor Constantine I established the Christian church as a very solid and accepted church throughout that part of the world. Sometime around the year 336 A.D., the Roman Empire decided to celebrate the anniversary of Jesus' birth, and chose December 25 as the date upon which to celebrate.

It was a joyful occasion for Christians when the rulers of the Roman Empire eventually accepted Christianity and the celebration of Christmas. Governments were not always so accepting of Christianity as a religion, and before

Constantine's rule, Christians were scorned, harassed, and sometimes even killed. Unfortunately, it was during a time of Christian persecution that a boy named Nicholas was born to Christian parents in the middle-eastern country of Lycia ...

Nicholas, a Young Christian

The idea of Santa Claus developed from stories about a real person named Saint Nicholas. Because Nicholas lived so long ago and we have very few written records that survive from that time in history, we know only a few facts, but records tell many stories about his life and work that many scholars agree must have some basis in truth. Here's what most scholars accept as generally true about Saint Nicholas:

He was born in Lycia (a country we now call Turkey) sometime around A.D. 280. Most sources agree that Nicholas' parents were wealthy Christians, and that Nicholas was a bright, curious boy who enjoyed learning about God and Jesus. Sadly, when he was eight years old, a plague swept through his hometown and killed both of his parents. Nicholas inherited their wealth; in comparison to other people of that time, the orphaned Nicholas was very rich. Nicholas was a shy, sensitive boy who often wandered around town by himself, and on these little journeys he began to realize how blessed he was in his wealth, and how many of his neighbors were suffering due to extreme poverty. Oftentimes he saw ragged children his own age begging for handouts of food and money. According to one source, Nicholas "would slip a coin into a beggar's hand and move on so quickly that the recipient would not learn Nicholas' identity." Nicholas did not want recognition or thanks; he simply felt brokenhearted about the needs of the poor, and he wanted to help them.

As he grew older, Nicholas devoted himself to learning more about his Christian faith. He studied Jesus' life and words, and was particularly impressed by Jesus' description of God's most important purposes for us. When Jesus' followers asked him what God most wanted them to do with their lives, He told them that God's wishes were as follows:

> *'You shall love the Lord your God with all your heart, and with all your soul, and with all your mind.' This is the great and foremost commandment. The second is like it, 'You shall love your neighbor as [much as you love] yourself.'*

Nicholas committed his own life to loving God completely and to showering love and care upon other people, especially the poor. Nicholas used up his entire inheritance helping needy, sick, and suffering people.

Many sources agree that Nicholas became a bishop (a high-ranking church leader) as a very young man. Some illustrations show Nicholas as a cardinal (another church leader), dressed all in red. He was imprisoned for a time because of his Christian faith, but was freed when Emperor Constantine I declared Christianity to be acceptable in the Roman Empire. Nicholas and his church members were now free to openly follow Jesus' commands, particularly by helping widows, orphans, and other unfortunate people who were cast aside by society. He especially cared about all children, and he tried to bring safety and love into the lives of the children who needed it most.

Sources also agree that much of Nicholas' giving was done, as in his early days, in secret; he did not want recognition or thanks, and he did not want recipients to feel that they owed him anything. In this matter he may have been following another of Jesus' commands:

> *When you give to the poor, do not let your left hand know what your right hand is doing, so that your giving will be in secret...*

Nicholas' widespread reputation as a loving man of God and a benefactor to children seems to be a fact that is confirmed by early records. Nicholas is believed to have died around A.D. 345, and within a century of his death he was celebrated as a saint. The anniversary of his death, December 6th, became a day of annual remembrance and celebration called St. Nicholas Day.

Saint Nicholas: The Legend

Although the *facts* about Saint Nicholas are few, the *legends* are many. Legends often stem from real, actual events, though they usually are embellished to make more interesting stories. Even if details about the events are not quite accurate, though, it's important to remember that legends which highlight a person's good qualities usually reflect the person's true nature.

Many of the St. Nicholas legends seem to contain truth interwoven with imagination. However, the following stories passed down through the centuries are considered to contain some part of historical truth. While the details might be exaggerated, Saint Nicholas' actions in these legends help us understand who he was and what he believed, and why he is so beloved and remembered as protector and helper of those in need.

The most commonly shared legend about Saint Nicholas involves a poor man who had three daughters. In those days, parents offered a gift, or "dowry," to the man who would marry their daughter. As you might expect, to attract a more "acceptable" husband, a girl's father would have to offer a respectable dowry. The poor man in this legend had no dowry to offer; since it didn't seem likely that his daughters would get married, he was sadly considering selling them into slavery.

When all seemed hopeless, a miracle occurred in the night: Three bags of gold were thrown through an open window. The bags landed in stockings or shoes that had been left by the fire to dry. The secret giver was Nicholas, and he did not want thanks or repayment; his gift was *unconditional*, which means he wanted nothing at all in return. He was simply modeling Jesus' commands to "love his neighbors" and to "give in secret." The family rejoiced; the girls would not be sold into slavery, and they would have dowries when the time came for them to marry.

This may be the first legend that portrays Saint Nicholas as a secret night visitor who leaves presents in stockings for children. Other legends describe events where Nicholas helps boys, sailors, and prisoners whose lives are threatened. Details vary, but a common theme in all the legends involves children and others whose wishes are fulfilled because of Saint Nicholas' compassion for them.

Following Saint Nicholas' example, Christians began honoring St. Nicholas (and therefore Jesus) by imitation, giving presents to people in need, as well as to loved ones, asking for no payment or gratitude in return. Moreover, children were told that if they were good, St. Nicholas would come secretly to fill their stockings or shoes in the dark, early hours of St. Nicholas Day. That's an idea that sounds familiar, doesn't it?

The Third Gift:

Living the Tradition

Saint Nicholas and Santa Claus

How did the kindly Christian saint, good Bishop Nicholas, become a roly-poly red-suited American symbol for merry holiday festivity and commercial activity? History tells the tale:

Throughout the hundreds and hundreds of years following the death of the real Saint Nicholas, legend and tradition ensured that his fame as a devotee of Jesus and a provider for children grew. By the 1400's, Christians in most countries in throughout Europe honored St. Nicholas on December 6th by giving gifts to children and loved ones, and also by showing charity to the poor and needy.

Holland, in particular, celebrated St. Nicholas and his beliefs, although his name there slowly transformed from Saint Nicholas to Sinter Klaas. When Dutch immigrants settled in the New York area of America in the 1600's, they brought their love for Sinter Klaas with them, and that nickname soon morphed into the name we know as Santa Claus.

To further confuse the holiday in America, settlers arriving from other parts of Europe brought with them an annual tradition of celebrating the birth of Jesus Christ on Christmas Day (December 25th). For several decades, the diverse, newly-settled Americans from various backgrounds celebrated in a variety of ways and on a variety of dates.

Two very popular literary works published in the 1800's helped transform Saint Nicholas into the Santa Claus that we know today. Author Washington Irving wrote a best-seller that described Saint Nicholas as a jolly man who wore a broad-brimmed hat and smoked a long pipe. Irving's Saint Nicholas rode over treetops in a wagon and filled children's stockings with presents. Then, on December 23, 1823, a poem by Clement Clarke Moore titled "An Account of a Visit from St. Nicholas" was published. In the poem, Saint Nicholas is described as a fat, smiling man with twinkling eyes and a red nose. He wears a suit trimmed with white fur, rides a sleigh pulled by eight reindeer, and sounds a lot like the man we call "Santa Claus" today. In the poem, Saint Nicholas' visit takes place on December 24th, a date popularly known as Christmas Eve.

In the decades since Moore's illustrated poem was published, the American idea of Saint Nicholas became more and more like the one we have of Santa Claus today. Unfortunately, remembrance of Saint Nicholas *the person* – the one who was devoted to a life serving God and modeling Jesus' commandments by loving and giving – faded. The holiday expanded somehow from a day that *celebrates God's gift of Jesus to humankind* to a day when *people give gifts to loved ones, mostly because it's fun to do so*. Many people lost the connection between Jesus' birth and Nicholas' reason for gift-giving, and nowadays it often seems that Christmas is two holidays combined: Some families continue the tradition of Santa's visit without event thinking about Jesus' birth; other families celebrate Jesus' birth but dismiss the Santa tradition as frivolous and greedy; still other some families celebrate both Jesus and Santa, perhaps not even thinking much about how the two may be connected, if at all.

Truly – and sadly, perhaps – if St. Nicholas were to visit America today, he would probably not recognize himself at all in the appearance or actions of Santa Claus. He would likely wonder why Santa gives so many *unneeded* gifts, why people often buy so much *stuff* that none of it seems special, and why the reason for Santa's gift-giving no longer points back through the centuries to the very first (and most important) gift: God's gift of Jesus to us all. Although Saint Nicholas always valued the joy of children, he would in all likelihood think that something *very important* is missing from the way most of us celebrate Christmas.

Can you step into Saint Nicholas' shoes and see his point-of-view? If so, how can we change the way we view Christmas so that we can do a better job of remembering and sharing the *real* "reason for the season"?

St. Nicholas' "Hands and Feet"

Christ has no body but yours,
No hands, no feet on earth but yours,
Yours are the eyes with which he looks Compassion on this world,
Yours are the feet with which he walks to do good,
Yours are the hands, with which he blesses all the world.
Yours are the hands, yours are the feet,
Yours are the eyes, you are his body.
Christ has no body now but yours,
No hands, no feet on earth but yours,
Yours are the eyes with which he looks compassion on this world.
Christ has no body now on earth but yours.

~Saint Teresa of Avila (1515-1582)

Saint Nicholas spent his life showing his love and gratitude to God by modeling Jesus' commandments – basically acting as Jesus' "hands and feet" - in his own place and time. He was devoted to God, thankful for God's gift of Jesus and Salvation available to all humankind, and anxious to teach others about Jesus by loving others, giving to those in need (especially children and poor neighbors), and making sure all of his good deeds pointed not to himself, but instead toward *God's* generosity, and to *Jesus'* commandments and love.

Now that we have learned more about Saint Nicholas (the man *and* the legend), what was important to him, and how his life inspired some of the traditions we associate with Christmas, we can take what we learned and add real meaning to the way we think about Christmas. Until now, perhaps, we have made lists, shopped, and waited for Christmas and the material gifts that Santa will bring; as an inspired observer has written, "Children spend the days and weeks before Christmas waiting for Santa Claus and the gifts he will bring—if they are good, that is. But St Nicholas says, no, you should be waiting for Someone Else at Christmas, the One who grants the gift of eternal life and all the other gifts of grace that help us attain our ultimate goal." Now we know we should be celebrating that Someone Else at Christmas, the

Christ Child who was born thousands of years ago but never died, whom Saint Nicholas spent his life honoring, whose message offers eternal life to those who believe and follow Him.

When God sent Jesus to earth to live among humans, Jesus served as God's "hands and feet" to physically show short-sighted humans who God is, and how He wants us to use our lives. He loved, fed, healed, and taught the people he met. He showed compassion toward sinners, even if their actions made them seem undeserving. He welcomed and loved the children, and understood how important they were in the world. He did good deeds and gave all glory not to Himself, but to God above. He suffered and gave up His life in exchange for forgiveness of the sins of ALL humankind, both those who lived in His day and those who live in ours. He taught His disciples how they should serve as His "hands and feet" by spreading His love and message throughout the world.

When Saint Nicholas – the real man – walked the earth, he dedicated his life to serving as Jesus' "hands and feet" by teaching others about Jesus, treasuring the children, giving generously and unconditionally to others, and giving all glory not to himself, but to God above. This was his ministry, and he would be pleased to know that after his death, others would serve as his "hands and feet" by copying his acts of generosity and compassion - and by spreading his message of God's gift and Jesus' love - throughout centuries.

And although our American celebration of Christmas today bears little resemblance to Saint Nicholas' actions and purpose, you can see that our gift-giving on the yearly anniversary of Jesus' birth is linked through time and tradition to Saint Nicholas' modeling of God's gift and message to us. When we give gifts *in honor and remembrance of Jesus' birth* – not out of materialism, or greed, or because stores tell us to, or just because almost everyone else does it – we ourselves are acting as Saint Nicholas' "hands and feet" by glorifying God and showing our gratitude for His greatest gift to us: Jesus.

Is Santa Claus real? If you are referring to a fat, jolly fellow dressed in red who (people say) comes down your chimney each year and leaves you toys... well, no. But the original Santa Claus, Saint Nicholas, is very much a real person who lived and breathed and walked the earth, modeling God's unconditional love and teaching about God's gift through Jesus to us. His actions were real, his tradition *is* real, and his message to you – and to all of us - is *real and everlasting*. So whenever your parents or other adults who love you have left gifts for you under the tree "from Santa," it is not part of some sneaky plot designed to fool you; instead, whether or not those adults realize it, they are taking part in a centuries-old tradition modeled by Saint Nicholas and inspired by God's gift to the world, and Jesus' example of how to give. Their gifts are unconditional, symbolizing God's love for you. Their gifts are left in secret, so the focus isn't on the giver but on the gifts themselves, which symbolize God's love and Jesus' sacrifice for you. Your parents are participating in an ancient and enduring tradition of acting as Saint Nicholas' "hands and feet," and I pray that you, yourself, will continue to appreciate and pass along Saint Nicholas' tradition as you live out the years of your own blessed life.

Paying It Forward: Operation Christmas Child

Just so you know, if you purchased the book that you are now reading, you have already done your part to carry forward Saint Nicholas' mission. A portion of the proceeds of this book is going to an international gift-giving project known as Operation Christmas Child.

Operation Christmas Child is a project run by a charitable organization called Samaritan's Purse, based in North Carolina. Every fall, the organizers of Operation Christmas Child ask for and receive millions (yes, MILLIONS) of donated gifts for children. Gifts typically include toys, school supplies, hygiene items, candy, and small clothing items. Operation Christmas Child packers then put the gifts in shoeboxes, wrap the shoeboxes in holiday wrap, and ship them to needy children all around the world.

I think that Saint Nicholas would be thrilled with this idea! By helping Operation Christmas Child through the purchase of this book (or supporting OCC by sending a donation and/or gifts for children), YOU TOO are acting as

Saint Nicholas' "hands and feet," furthering his mission to demonstrate God's love for His children in a practical, helpful way.

To learn more about *Operation Christmas Child,* **visit** *www.samaritanspurse.org*

"Santa & St. Nicholas"

Santa Claus is round and plump;
St. Nicholas is tall and thin.

Santa Claus wears a stocking cap;
St. Nicholas wears a bishop's hat.

Santa Claus comes December 25th;
St. Nicholas comes December 6th.

Santa Claus is often seen in stores;
St. Nicholas is often seen in churches.

Santa Claus flies through the air—from the North Pole;
St. Nicholas walked the earth, caring for those in need.

Santa Claus, for some, replaces Jesus at Christmas;
St. Nicholas, for all, points to Jesus at Christmas.

Santa Claus isn't bad;
St. Nicholas is just better!

—C. Myers & J. Rosenthal
St. Nicholas Center
www.stnicholascenter.org

NOTES

INTRODUCTION and CHAPTER 1: THE VERY FIRST CHRISTMAS

PAGE

4   "A very good attempt..." Church, Francis Pharcellus. "Yes, Virginia, There Is a Santa Claus," *Newseum.*

12   "For a child will be born..." *New American Standard Bible,* Isaiah 9:6-7, pp. 971-2.

13   "While they were there..." *New American Standard Bible,* Luke 2:6-11; pp. 1462-3.

18   "For Christ also died..." *New American Standard Bible,* I Peter 3:18, p. 1817.

19   "For God so loved the world..." *New American Standard Bible,* John 3:16, p. 1520.

19   "I am the resurrection..." *New American Standard Bible,* John 11:25-6, p. 1540.

CHAPTER 2: SAINT NICHOLAS

PAGE

23   "The Emperor of the vast and all-powerful..." "Constantine the Great," *ReligionFacts.*

23   "Sometime around the year 336 A.D..." Myers, R.J., "Christmas." *World Book Advanced.*

24   "The idea of Santa Claus..." Myers, R.J., "Santa Claus," *World Book Advanced.*

24   "He was born..." "St. Nicholas Biography," *The Biography Channel website.*

24   "Most sources agree..." Myers, Carol, "Who is St. Nicholas?" *St. Nicholas Center.*

25   "Sadly, when he was eight..." Jeffers, H. Paul, p. 20

26   "As he grew older..." Wheeler, Joe, p. 6

26	"You shall love the Lord your God…" *New American Standard Bible*, Matt. 22:37-9.
26	"Nicholas used up…" Myers, Carol, "Who is St. Nicholas?" *St. Nicholas Center*.
26	"Many sources agree…" Myers, R.J., "Santa Claus."
27	"He was imprisoned for a time…" Gruen, Erich S. "Constantine the Great," *World Book Advanced*.
27	"Nicholas and his church members…" Cann, D.L., p. 10.
27	"He especially cared about all children…" Bevilacqua and Toropov, *The Everything Christmas Book*, p. 251.
27	"… much of Nicholas' giving was done…" Wheeler, p. 11.
28	"When you give to the poor…" *New American Standard Bible*, Matthew 6:3-4, p. 1376.
28	"Nicholas is believed to have died…" Myers, Carol, "Who is St. Nicholas?" *St. Nicholas Center*.
29	"Many of the St. Nicholas legends seem…" Ibid.
29	"The most commonly shared legend…" "St. Nicholas Biography," *The Biography Channel website*.
31	"Following Saint Nicholas' example…" Wheeler, p. 53.
31	"Moreover, children were told…" Jeffers, p. 34.

CHAPTER 3: LIVING THE TRADITION

PAGE

34	"Holland, in particular, celebrated… " Bevilacqua & Toropov, *The Everything Christmas Book*, p. 253.
34	"When Dutch immigrants settled…" Jeffers, p. 43
35	"To further confuse the holiday…" Ibid.
35	"Two very popular literary works…" Myers, R.J., "Santa Claus."
35	"Then, on December 23, 1823, a poem by Clement Clarke Moore…" Ibid.
36	"In the decades since…" Seal, Jeremy.
37	"Truly – and sadly, perhaps…." Bevilacqua & Toropov, p. 258.

39	"Christ has no body but yours…" St. Teresa of Avila (quoted by Daniel B. Clendenin).
40	"Until now, perhaps,…" Homick, Fr. Joseph, "St. Nicholas and the Coming of the Lord," *Making All Things New.*
44	"Operation Christmas Child is a project…" "Operation Christmas Child," *Samaritan's Purse.*
47	"Santa & St. Nicholas," Rosenthal, J., & C. Myers, *St. Nicholas Center.*

BIBLIOGRAPHY

Bevilacqua, Michelle, and Brandon Toropov, General Editors. *The Everything Christmas Book*. Holbrook MA: The Adams Media Corporation, 1994.

Cann, D. L. *Saint Nicholas, Bishop of Myra: The Life and Times of the Original Father Christmas*. Ottawa: Novalis, 2002.

Church, Francis Pharcellus. "Yes, Virginia, there is a Santa Claus." *Newseum*. Accessed December 7, 2012. http://newseum.org/yesvirginia/.

"Constantine the Great." *ReligionFacts*. Accessed October 8, 2012. http://www.religionfacts.com/christianity/people/constantine.htm.

Gruen, Erich S. "Constantine the Great." *World Book Advanced*. Accessed July 7, 2013. http://worldbookonline.com/advanced/article?id=ar130820&st=constantine+i.

Homick, Fr. Joseph. *Making All Things New* (blog). http://wordincarnate.wordpress.com/2010/12/06/st-nicholas-and-the-coming-of-the-lord/.

Jeffers, H. Paul. *Legends of Santa Claus (A&E Biography)*. Minneapolis: Lerner Publications Company, 2001.

Myers, Carol. "Who Is St. Nicholas?" *St. Nicholas Center.* Accessed August 19, 2012, http://www.stnicholascenter.org/pages/who-is-st-nicholas/.

Myers, R.J. "Santa Claus." *World Book Advanced.* Accessed November 4, 2011. http://worldbookonline.com/advanced/article?id=ar489960.

Myers, R.J. "Christmas." World Book Advanced. Accessed November 4, 2011. http://worldbookonline.com/advanced/article?id=ar113660&st=christmas.

"Operation Christmas Child." *Samaritan's Purse.* Accessed June 28, 2013. http://www.samaritanspurse.org/what-we-do/operation-christmas-child/.

Rosenthal, J., and C. Myers. "Santa Claus & St. Nicholas." *St. Nicholas Center.* Accessed June 27, 2013. http://www.stnicholascenter.org/pages/compare-santa-st-nicholas/.

Saint Teresa of Avila. "Christ Has No Body." *Journey with Jesus* (webzine, Daniel B. Clendenin, author and editor). Accessed November 17, 2012. http://www.journeywithjesus.net/PoemsAndPrayers/Teresa_Of_Avila_Christ_Has_No_Body.shtml.

Seal, Jeremy. "The Story of St. Nicholas: Interview with Jeremy Seal." By Renee Montagne. *NPR.com*. December 23, 2005. http://www.npr.org/templates/story/story.php?storyId=5067257.

"St. Nicholas Biography." *The Biography Channel website*. Accessed September 12, 2012. http://www.biography.com/people/st-nicholas-204635.

St. Nicholas Center. *Saint Nicholas Center*. Accessed August 19, 2012. http://www.stnicholascenter.org/pages/home/.

Wheeler, Joe. *Christian Encounters: Saint Nicholas*. Nashville, TN: Thomas Nelson, Inc., 2010.

Made in the USA
Middletown, DE
01 December 2016